★ HOCKEY SUPERSTARS ★

JOHN TAVARES

BY SHANE FREDERICK

CAPSTONE PRESS
a capstone imprint

Sports Illustrated Kids Hockey Superstars are published by Capstone Press,
1710 Roe Crest Drive, North Mankato, Minnesota 56003.
www.capstonepub.com

Library of Congress Cataloging-in-Publication Data
Frederick, Shane.
John Tavares / by Shane Frederick.
pages cm. — (Sports illustrated kids. Hockey superstars.)
Includes bibliographical references and index.
Summary: "Details the life and career of hockey superstar John Tavares"—Provided by publisher.
ISBN 978-1-62065-158-2 (library binding)
ISBN 978-1-4914-9025-9 (paperback)
ISBN 978-1-4914-7606-2 (eBook PDF)
1. Tavares, John, 1990—Juvenile literature. 2. Hockey players—United States—Biography—Juvenile literature. 3. Hockey players—Canada—Biography—Juvenile literature. I. Title.
GV848.5.T38F74 2016
796.962092—dc23
[B] 2015006649

Editorial Credits
Brenda Haugen, editor; Terri Poburka, designer; Eric Gohl, media researcher; Tori Abraham, production specialist

Photo Credits
Dreamstime: Jerry Coli, 1, 15, 27, 30–31 (background), 32 (background), Jwong526, cover; Getty Images: Bruce Bennett, 4, 25, Claus Andersen, 19, Richard Wolowicz, 10, Stringer/Dave Abel, 14, 17; Newscom: Icon SMI/Rick Denham, 8, Icon Sportswire CGV/Rich Graessle, 29, Reuters/Shannon Stapleton, 23, Reuters/Shaun Best, 20, ZUMA Press/Toronto Star/Salvatore Sacco, 13; Sports Illustrated: John Iacono, 7
Design Elements: Shutterstock

Printed in the United States of America in North Mankato, Minnesota.
032015 008823CGF15

TABLE OF CONTENTS

Reebok
Reebok
Reebok
12
29
EASTON

CHAPTER 1

A NEW HOPE

The New York Islanders and Pittsburgh Penguins were knotted up midway through the third period of a 2013 playoff game. The Islanders' Brad Boyes stole the puck from an opposing player, and he knew what to do with it. **Center** John Tavares may have been only 22 years old, but he was already one of the best offensive players in the National Hockey League (NHL).

Tavares caught the pass from Boyes as he skated toward the net. Moving the puck from his backhand to his forehand and back to his backhand, Tavares took his shot. The goaltender made the first save, but Tavares was there to knock the rebound in the net.

The Nassau Veterans Memorial Coliseum fans were in a frenzy. The highlight-reel goal put the Islanders ahead for good. There was finally some hope again for the hockey team on Long Island.

center—the player who participates in a face-off at the beginning of play

The New York Islanders were the best team in the NHL in the early 1980s. They were a group of stars. Tough, high-scoring skaters such as Mike Bossy, Bryan Trottier, and Denis Potvin thrilled fans and led the team to four **Stanley Cup** championships in a row.

Then times got tough. Over the next 25 years, the Islanders enjoyed just 10 seasons in which they won as many or more games than they lost. Good players came and went, but the Islanders needed a new superstar who might lead them back to greatness.

The Islanders had the No. 1 overall pick in the **draft** in the summer of 2009. They chose a player they hoped could one day lead them to glory. That talented, high-scoring forward was named John Tavares.

FAST FACT

The Islanders are one of only two NHL teams to win at least four Stanley Cups in a row. The other is the Montreal Canadiens. The Canadiens won five straight Stanley Cups from 1956 to 1960 and four in a row from 1976 to 1979.

Stanley Cup—**the trophy given each year to the NHL champion**

draft—**the process of choosing a person to join a sports organization or team**

Bryan Trottier lifts the Stanley Cup in 1983.

RBK
11
A
SENE

CHAPTER 2

NATURAL BORN SCORER

John Tavares was born September 20, 1990, in Mississauga, Ontario, Canada. Mississauga is located on the shore of Lake Ontario near Canada's largest city, Toronto. John's family moved to Oakville, another Toronto suburb, when he was young.

John fell in love with sports at a young age. He learned to play soccer, lacrosse, and hockey. Hockey was his favorite sport, though. He took his first lesson at age 3, and he immediately tried to skate with the big kids. After that it didn't take long for people to figure out he was a natural.

AN ATHLETIC FAMILY

John's uncle, who shares the name John Tavares, is also a pro athlete. The older Tavares plays lacrosse. He is the all-time leading scorer in the National Lacrosse League, an indoor lacrosse league in North America. He has been an important influence on his nephew, teaching him to be an unselfish player and a good teammate. When the younger Tavares was a kid, he served as the ball boy for his uncle's team, the Buffalo Bandits.

John poses with his parents, Barb and Joe, at an awards gala in Quebec, Canada, in 2009.

As a youth player, John wasn't just good at hockey. He was the best in his age group in Canada. As a 6-year-old, he scored the championship-winning goal in a big postseason tournament in the Canadian capital of Ottawa. He also was named the tournament's most valuable player (MVP).

The next year John moved up a level and played with and against older kids. He was still one of the best players on the ice. That continued to be the case as he grew up.

As a 13-year-old bantam, John scored 95 goals and racked up 187 **points** in 90 games. The next season at the midget level, he had 91 goals and 158 points in just 72 games. He moved up another notch to a league that included players as old as 20 while he was just 14. He played there the rest of the season.

On that team, the Milton Icehawks, John continued to show off his supreme skills. In just 20 games, he scored 13 goals and had 28 points. Where could he go next?

points—a player's total number of goals and assists

John wanted to play at the major junior level, specifically the Ontario Hockey League (OHL). There was just one problem. When the 2005 OHL draft came along, he was only 14 years old. The OHL had a rule that required players to be 16 years old. Tavares wouldn't even turn 15 for four months.

Tavares' request was denied at first, just as NHL superstars Sidney Crosby's and Mario Lemieux's requests were denied by the Quebec Major Junior Hockey League in previous years. However the OHL reconsidered. The OHL took into account John's statistics and his size. He was already 6 feet, 1 inch (185.4 centimeters) tall and 180 pounds (81.6 kilograms). The league let him in under a new "exceptional player" status for top athletes.

With the first pick in the draft, the Oshawa Generals selected the young Tavares. And he didn't disappoint.

GENERALS
OSHAWA'S
1350CKDO
ROGERS

CCM
Oshawa
GENERAL
91
CCM
CCM

On September 23, 2005, three days after turning 15 years old, John suited up for the Generals. Being the youngest player on the rink was nothing new to John, but now he was sharing the ice with top NHL **prospects**. Many of those players were bigger and stronger than John was. They weren't going to take it easy on him, even if he was considered exceptional.

prospect—a person who is likely to play pro hockey

Bobby Orr scoring a goal

YOUNG GUNS

John Tavares wasn't the youngest player to skate in the major junior leagues. He followed in two other players' footsteps. Bobby Orr was 14 when he signed with the NHL's Boston Bruins in 1962 and was assigned to the Oshawa Generals. In 1968 Denis Potvin, who went on to greatness with the New York Islanders, played his first junior games at the age of 14.

CHAPTER 3

"THE NEXT ONE"

Just as he had at every other level of hockey, Tavares shined against the older players. He scored a goal on his first shot in his first game for Oshawa and tallied 10 points in his first nine games. Coach Randy Ladouceur had kept Tavares on the ice a lot and in every situation, including **power plays** and **penalty kills**.

At the end of the season, Tavares had proven he belonged. He scored 45 goals and 77 points in 65 games. He was named the **Rookie** of the Year by the Canadian Hockey League (CHL).

FAST FACT

The Canadian Hockey League oversees 60 teams that make up three major leagues, including the Ontario Hockey League, the Quebec Major Junior Hockey League, and the Western Hockey League.

power play—**when a team has a one- or two-player advantage because the other team has one or more players in the penalty box**

penalty kill—**when a team plays short-handed because a player is in the penalty box**

rookie—**a first-year player**

CCM
31

Tavares had become the Generals' main attraction. His popularity drew comparisons to two other Oshawa players who went on to NHL stardom following their junior careers: Eric Lindros and Bobby Orr. During his second season in the OHL, Tavares began getting compared to another great player—the greatest hockey player of all time, Wayne Gretzky.

During the 1977–78 season, Gretzky played for the OHL's Sault Ste. Marie Greyhounds. He scored 70 goals, the league record for a 16-year-old. Twenty-nine years later, Tavares broke that record by racking up 72 goals!

Tavares also had 62 assists during the 2006–07 season to finish with 134 points. He was the easy pick for CHL Player of the Year. Tavares also received another unofficial title that season, The Next One, a play on Gretzky's nickname, The Great One.

FAST FACT

Wayne Gretzky holds or shares 61 NHL records, many of which may never be broken. He is the league's all-time leader in goals (894) and assists (1,962). His assist total alone would keep him the NHL's career point-scoring leader.

91
GENERALS
CCM
Oshawa
GENERALS
BAUER

CANADA

Tavares continued to dominate the OHL the next season. He scored 40 more goals and added 118 points during the regular season. He thought he was ready for the NHL, and a few NHL teams thought he was ready too. But once again his age got in his way. Tavares was too young to be drafted by an NHL team, but he hoped the league would make an exception for him, just as the OHL did. The league stood its ground and told him he would have to wait.

Tavares returned to the OHL for a fourth year. Midway through that season, he played for Team Canada in the World Junior Championship. He led his home country to a gold medal and was named tournament MVP after scoring eight goals and 15 points in six games.

After the World Championship, Oshawa said goodbye to Tavares and traded him to the London Knights. With the Knights Tavares scored his 214th OHL goal, breaking a 33-year-old record. He finished his major junior career with 215 goals and 433 points.

CHAPTER 4

TAVARES' ISLAND

Tavares was finally old enough, and more than ready, for the NHL. When the 2009 draft came around, he was considered to be the top forward prospect because of all he accomplished in the OHL and in **international** competition.

The New York Islanders, who had the worst record in the NHL in 2008–09, had the No. 1 overall selection. More than 10,000 Islanders fans flocked to Nassau Coliseum to watch a broadcast of the draft. The Islanders hadn't won a playoff series in 16 seasons. The fans hoped that the Islanders would take a player who could help make the team great again.

They cheered wildly when Tavares' name was announced as the pick.

FAST FACT

Tavares is one of four No. 1 overall draft picks taken by the New York Islanders. The others were wing Billy Harris in 1972, defenseman Denis Potvin in 1973, and goaltender Rick DiPietro in 2000.

international—including more than one nation

wing—a type of forward who usually stays near the sides of the zone

NHL
NY
ISLANDERS

Expectations were high for Tavares. Fans hoped he really was "The Next One." They also saw how other recent No. 1 picks, such as the Pittsburgh Penguins' Sidney Crosby, the Washington Capitals' Alex Ovechkin, and the Chicago Blackhawks' Patrick Kane, were helping their teams win.

Tavares lived up to expectations. His knack for putting pucks in the net and making plays for teammates to do the same carried over from the junior level to the big leagues. Tavares played in his first NHL game October 3, 2009. He and his teammates faced the defending Stanley Cup-champion Penguins. Although the Islanders lost in a **shoot-out** that night, Tavares showed he belonged by scoring a goal and assisting on another.

Tavares finished his first season with 54 points, including 24 goals, in 82 games. He ranked second in the league that season in points among first-year players, just behind Matt Duchene of the Colorado Avalanche. After the season Tavares was named to the NHL's All-Rookie Team.

shoot-out—a method of breaking a tie score at the end of overtime play

ISLANDERS
CCM
24

Tavares led the Islanders in scoring in each of his first four NHL seasons. As a second-year player, he recorded his first **hat trick**. He also showed off his magical hands. He scored 29 goals and 67 points in 79 games during the 2010–11 season.

The next season the Islanders were convinced Tavares would be the player to turn their luck around. Five days before Tavares turned 21 years old, the team signed him to a six-year, $33 million contract extension. He also was named an alternate captain.

Tavares responded with his best season yet. He scored 31 goals and assisted on 50 others and was named to the All-Star Team. His 81 points ranked seventh in the NHL.

The 2012–13 season was shortened due to a contract dispute between NHL team owners and players. When the season finally began, Tavares could not be stopped. In 48 games he scored 28 goals, which ranked third in the league. More important, he also led the Islanders into the playoffs for the first time in six years.

hat trick—**a feat achieved by a hockey player who scores three goals in one game**

CCM
91
A
NY

After the 2012–13 season, Tavares was named a finalist for the Hart Trophy, which goes to the NHL's most valuable player. The other candidates were Ovechkin and Crosby, and Ovechkin won. But just as he'd always done, the 22-year-old Tavares proved he deserved a place among the league's top players.

The next season the Islanders stitched a "C" on Tavares' jersey, making him their captain. He was the second-youngest captain in the league at the time. He was definitely the superstar Islanders fans had been waiting for.

Tavares played for Team Canada in the 2014 Olympics in Sochi, Russia. Canada took home the gold medal that year, but it was bittersweet for Tavares. He suffered a knee injury. It not only caused him to miss the Olympic semifinals and final, but it ended his NHL season too. At the time he ranked third in the league in scoring with 66 points.

Tavares quickly proved he was fully recovered during the 2014–15 season. He racked up 70 points in the first 67 games to lead the NHL. Fans have high hopes that Tavares will soon lead the Islanders to another Stanley Cup victory.

FAST FACT

The Islanders decided to move from the Nassau Coliseum in Uniondale, New York, making the newer Barclays Center in Brooklyn, New York, their home beginning in the 2015–16 season.

CCM
NY
C
ISLANDERS

GLOSSARY

center (SEN-tur)—the player who participates in a face-off at the beginning of play

draft (DRAFT)—the process of choosing a person to join a sports organization or team

hat trick (HAT TRIK)—a feat achieved by a hockey player who scores three goals in one game

international (in-tur-NASH-uh-nuhl)—including more than one nation

penalty kill (PEN-uhl-tee KIL)—when a team plays short-handed because a player is in the penalty box

points (POYNTZ)—a player's total number of goals and assists

power play (POW-ur PLAY)—when a team has a one- or two-player advantage because the other team has one or more players in the penalty box

prospect (PRAHS-pekt)—a person who is likely to play pro hockey

rookie (RUK-ee)—a first-year player

shoot-out (SHOOT-owt)—a method of breaking a tie score at the end of overtime play

Stanley Cup (STAN-lee KUP)—the trophy given each year to the NHL champion

wing (WING)—a type of forward who usually stays near the sides of the zone

READ MORE

Frederick, Shane. *The Ultimate Collection of Pro Hockey Records.* Sports Illustrated Kids: For the Record. North Mankato, Minn.: Capstone Press, 2013.

Gitlin, Marty. *Hockey.* Minneapolis: ABDO Pub., 2012.

Jordan, Christopher. *We Are the Goal Scorers: The Top Point Leaders of the NHL.* New York: Fenn/Tundra, 2013.

INTERNET SITES

FactHound offers a safe, fun way to find Internet sites related to this book. All of the sites on FactHound have been researched by our staff.

Here's all you do:

Visit *www.facthound.com*

Type in this code: 9781620651582

Check out projects, games and lots more at **www.capstonekids.com**

INDEX